ZERO
READERSHIP

ACKNOWLEDGEMENTS:

Much thanks to the people of Belgrade

to the Marinovich family

to longtime friends Julien Poirier, Yelena Gluzman, Alicia Rabins, Elizabeth Reddin, Anna Moschovakis, Matvei Yankelevich, Ellie Ga, Illya Bernstein, Greg Ford, Jacqueline Waters, Amanda Strang, David Morgan Sollors, Karen Lillis, Dora King, Greg Houser, Greta Goetz, Genya Turovskaya, Nathaniel Farrell, Nathaniel Siegel, Dusko Vuckovic, Vesna Furundzic, and many many more, and to Karen Weiser and Anselm Berrigan near the top of the Akropolis July 2005 by surprise

to teachers Timothy Donnelly, Alan Ziegler, Matthew Lippman, Milosh Marinovich, Frank Lima, Alice Notley, Michael Golston, Marjorie Welish, Lucie Brock-Broido, Richard Howard, Mary Jo Bang, Michael Taussig, Bob Holman, Kristin Prevallet, Margo Jefferson, Ron Padgett

to students in the workshops where pieces from this work were first performed

to Corrine Fitzpatrick, Stacy Szymazek and Arlo Quint at The Poetry Project at St. Marks Church, Sara Marcus at Dixon Place, Tim Peterson, Stephen Paul Miller, and Cecilia Wu at Critiphoria, The West End, Julien Poirier at New York Nights, Lerner Hall where pieces from this work were first x-rayed and played

to the amazing people of the New York City Poetry Friendship Carnival Against Gentrification and War and For Art and More Life

Thank you
FM

* *

Cover and interior drawings by Filip Marinovich
Design by Don't Look Now!

ISBN: 1-933254-43-2
ISBN-13: 978-1-933254-43-2

Cataloging-in-publication data is available from the Library of Congress

First Edition, 2008

Ugly Duckling Presse
at the Old American Can Factory
232 Third St. #E002
Brooklyn, NY 11215
www.uglyducklingpresse.org

Distributed by Small Press Distribution
1341 Seventh Street
Berkeley, CA 94710
www.spdbooks.org

ZERO READERSHIP

an epic

by Filip Marinovich

DEDICATED TO
LILLIAN, NASH AND AL
NADA AND MILOS
ZORANA AND ZORA

IN LOVING MEMORY OF
MILOS MARINOVIC
1913-2007

```
****************************************************************
```

TIMESPACE:

```
****************************************************************
```

PROLOG

Belgrade, Yugoslavia
July 2001

BELGRADE EYES

limbs on a church roof
the client on the bed in the cemetery
the folksinger dealt to the mob and protested over
with a red broomstick, a red railway in the sky...

Find whatever you know and go get the red
handkerchief dropped by the astronaut onto Earth
for he searched to see if chivalry still existed on the planet
Earth planet Earth is red and a mushroom smile.

Who are you railing against on the terrace railing when you jump
five flights down into your courtyard near a church roof
strewn with legs from the television station bombed for broadcasting
the bombing of Belgrade.

"If she couldn't with her reason and intellect live
through it, then how can we, what's left for us?"
                                   Who are you to sing the dead you never knew?
The skulls in the sky were not clouds but calcified jugglers

and parrot mouths without a beak.
The mutant is a mainstay in Belgrade
let the mutant into the new minority sector
the radioactive child radios in for Mayday

is his birthday and Crash the name of his son.
The rage does nothing, aunt crying on a couch
has a couch to cry on, aunts underground
sprout tricolor plants through the terrace.

Who asks you how you can sleepwalk across the street
when you see a people moving on tractors
with all their possessions packed in garbage bags
and the breadline smokes--

When you fought against
the invisible, who cried out
and found you at the bottom of a well
and cast nets for your recovery...

                        --and underground bread smokes...
you feel faint on the street, smile at the bookseller
who sells complete editions to keep a small percentage
of his head. The cranial sack is taken camping

and nothing is lost. "You want me to help you
'liberate' the country? *You* uncork the grenade with your teeth--
we don't have a hundred lives. Who christened you
the leader of a nation to send boys in sacks home?

When The Old Man returns we will have cake to eat
and bread from fields the dead fertilize
barefoot on the cobbles hosed down by streetcleaners.
Remember, Century, The Old Man left

to blow out the blowtorch when the controls got busted
by a pack of missiles from the sky-----
we thought it was lightning until the little bombs dropped out

on parachutes-----a big black thing laid eggs all over the sky
hatching explosion chicks on the ground to vibrations of
the earth packed with Uranium Array and re-packed..."

With the soap on TV she sat on the couch
and cried because she could not take
twelve years of this--

twelve years of this but nothing
wrists slashed
but twelve years of this
and you, "clean like a tear,"

                              stopped up a sink.
                    She jumped from the fifth flight
into her courtyard into twelve years of
        jumping into no time and never returning--

the years starve--baby on highchair--Space!
Twelve years of this and falling into the pit
  --the aunt waiting but not crying, playing a game
of words with the cousin you know but don't know who lives in Budapest

because of twelve years--swamp with a Yugoslav flag stuck in it.
    Still a well sucks up all the fat
on your body and hoists it up in buckets at the hands of the well-keeper
drunk on plum brandy and the stinging red beards

of militia   and the hollow shell of a building--

years of

                                          no evidence
to try the bombers with because the evidence all bombed.

And radiated the ground, the bread,
the underground for twelve years of these

tryouts tomorrow for death

a leg on the roof, a pan for a shield,
leaves turn the corner and you bring coffee
        grandfather coughing behind a newspaper
a box of buttons under the coffee table.

BOOK 1:

ELGRADE EXSTATICS / WOLFMAN LANCE / SINGIDUNUM BLUES

7/19/05 - 8/10/05
Belgrade, Serbia and Montenegro

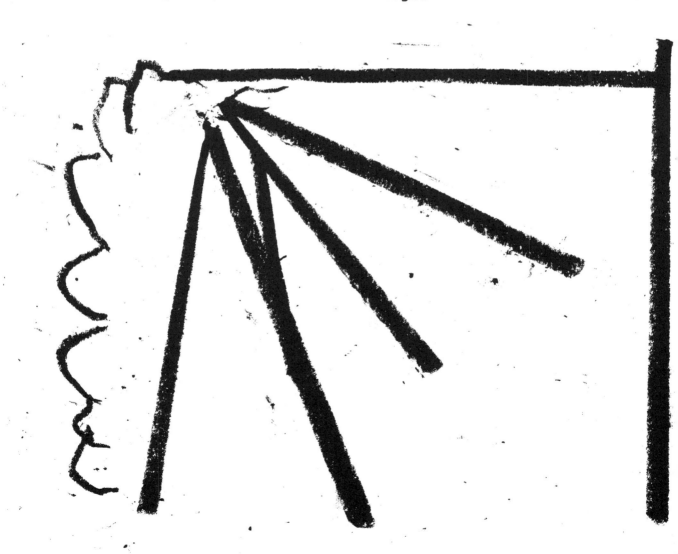

EXTENDED FAMILY VOICES

four black suitcases against the china cupboard.
what did she pack them for? "We're going!--"

I am a super communicative electric shepherd
hidden beneath the grass I shock the dog who wanders beyond
the property's threshold.
                              What did she pack? everything for the sea.
"But where is that rainjacket I bought in Switzerland? Mercy
will kill me."   i
                         n
                         j
                         a
                    stars

                                   hit me in my sciatic nerve.
                         I saw them older than last time old.
The cabbie dropped me five blocks from where I wanted to go.

          "Afternoons we reminisce--childhood--
                    we pack the suitcases and drag them around
          on hardwood floors till we see tracks."

Four black suitcases against the china cupboard.
"You are not my husband you are my father, don't show that ID card
to anyone, they'll report you as a forger.
                                   What house am I in--
          I know the days--Monday Toofsday Way--
     precious little to me...pass the honeydew melon. This one's esp-
     ecially sweet."

I am super conservative when it comes to space station hygeine

all my pets follow me into ark bath.

We are utensils to be rinsed and rerinsed at temperatures above
                         one hundred one--what--
Farenheit out the door with the interphone ringing

7/19/05

elephant
welcome

                    Belgrade roosters
                                screaming from beyond zoo wall

*   *   *   *   *   *   *   *   *   *   *   *   *

aziote
        tranzit

tranzit chips

tranzit

*

wind shuts the door.

*

Belgrade

a wreath

four black suitcases lined up against the china cupboard

ORIGIN in white lettering down their sides

where are we going?

ancestor ancestor what is an ancestor?

_____

                                                    7/20/05

DEAR A

                    my connecting flight to Belgrade shaking
God grabbed the plane with his sandbox hands
and banged it from behind with his stormcloud cock
I practiced doggystyle breaths strapped into my seat
prayed for the clay chess pieces I would make if we landed
repented, joined the armed forces, converted
to an oxygenated green religion I invented and forgot to name
where I was already dead and could die in no plane.
We landed at Belgrade airport to the screams of babygirl twins
behind me--actually only one screamed, the other remained silent
I didn't even know they were twins until we landed,
I nearly lied to you here, please forgive, I can't go back and
retake that same walk to the head of the table and change it.
I use these crayons without naming the colors they give.
What crayons? If I'd named them I would now remember where I placed them
for safekeeping. Crayon safety is important in this cave.

I meet exstatics every day here who speak to me of how to await bombers,
stealth bombers, by throwing a roof party or standing on your terrace
with a wooden bowl of freshly washed plums and shaking your finger
wet with plum juice and spit at the sky as it hums and releases
green tomahawk flashes students write their homework by. My aunt Milena
came over and made what's called Turkish coffee here and Greek coffee
in Greece and we sat on the terrace and drank it as Gramma Nada
repeated the same questions over and over   --a talk fugue.
"Do you have a woman? Where are the women who slept here last night?
When are we going to the seacoast? We are here a few more days and
then   going going going where?   to the sea and
two weeks there and two weeks the mountains. Do you have a woman?"
She packs her black suitcases every day and wheels them to the china
cabinet before the front door--ORIGIN--written in faded white
lettering down each of their four sides. Outside at Skadarlija
bohemian quarter Wolfman and I walk the dancing chips between
the beer gardens. All five tables are reserved under these lindens
so we go to Red Bar for draft beer and "conversations of real use."

New signs are up since I was last here, place names with
English translations--"Student's Park", "Bohemian Quarter", "Belgrade
Cathedral"--in English they all sound non-existent. English floats
up in treetops, a rootbeer float poured into a bird's nest
Serbian bubbles in roots and breaks from bark

if I drink this glass of homemade red. Nada's nurse Snowy
wants to set me up with her 25 year old daughter. I am 29
with a love for pink waterbottle caps Nada's black suitcases and
the necksuck Grampa Mercy gives me, surprised to see me in his hallways
before he stumbles to bed with his artificial right hip and the cough
that makes me think he will die any second, I can't witness that, I breathe
on the couch--kneel and pray to Holy Mother Three Hands
for the health of myself, family and world. Her white and gold
icon glistens on the wall by the mirror and the glass vase with sunflowers
bowing in it. Applause! Encore! "If you pray in space you are not there."
I am not in space but Belgrade, I suspect you sense this. "You suspect
everything!" says Wolfman. We finish our beers and he walks me home
the long way. "Chaos, craziness, cunts, in the rhythm we go!" as K says.
I ask Wolfman up to the balcony for a beer but he goes home.
I open the door and Grampa Mercy is reading obituaries by living

room lamplight. I am indeed still in the city--A--
a Roman tourgroup follows a blonde tourguide and her sign to a beergarden
on dancing chips. "You look strengthened" says Wolfman when we meet
at Republic Square.

                    "In '99 Belgraders held rock concerts there
in the midst of the NATO bombing campaign. Everything was great
during the day, nobody went to school, special plays were made for
kids in all the theaters."

                    "We shook our sweet plumprobing fingers
at the blue and white spring sky knowing at night it would spit
green tomahawk flashes down at us."

                        "For early curfew
I went home and did my homework as a tomahawk blew by my window."

    "I couldn't sleep and the radio was on in every room. Do-wop groups
and news was all I listened to, I still do.
                                Oh my friend,
it's easy for you, difficult for the intelligent."

                                Uncle Walrus
smiles at me from across his kitchen table while we deliberate
on what kind of pies my sisters and I should get: spinach, cherry or
cherry blossom. The three of us gorgeous chicks cause spontaneous orgasms
in the street when we walk the dancing chips and listen to roosters
cry out behind Belgrade Zoo walls and catch a cab
to Captain Mouse Street, Housepainter Street and
Revolution Boulevard where Iva's going with the dark green Che Guevara
        tattoo on her left shoulderblade.

I can drink as much coffee as I want here and feel alert
not panicky. "So many people are afraid of making shit
they make nothing, so you say to yourself So I'll make shit
so what, and you do it and see how impossible it is for you--
even if you want to--you would make shit if you painted still lifes
to sell for 59 dinars on Prince Mercy Street." Above the balcony
blackbirds shoot past the faded stone clock on the Paratrooper's
Club building. I can drink as much coffee--and I want the daybreak
to blow holes in me with no gun, just the way it looks at me from
all angles   if I   stare it in the eyes I   have to
                   whirl whirl on the balcony and imitate the
planet colder this July for the extra gas blown into it
by driving to the supermarket for milk, cantaloupes and corn. I will go
out there now and whirl and if you find me in the morning stretched out bel-
ow, thank the paratroopers the blackbirds and the bright blue
watergun heaven for tempting me over the flimsy black plastic edge
with its flowerpots the orange Peacelover grows from
with the black flies.

Who says I will be stretched out? I will land on Captain Mouse street
feet first and dance to the Belgrade Zoo and cry out with the roosters
at four in the morning and throw them out of their cages over the
brick walls and free every giraffe elephant and raccoon
                   the tigers the baboons the ostriches
                                          all sentient beings
dancing on the dancing ships of the flooded street. Let each typo
in my letter to you, Universe, be a pilot that flies me to my true
secret desire, the lotus petals spit from the slotmachine,
K touching her shoulder to mine in the taxi to the Greek embassy,
      Natalia waking
                   in her drunk father's arms at 2AM and crying
at the German shepherd he shows her.

                             Grampa Mercy coughs in his bed
am I disturbing him with all these empty threats to whirl on the balc-
ony until I drill a tunnel deep into mass grave earth and
identify my ancestors by the birthmarks in their eyes that I have--
their eyes   still intact they wake and follow me to the zoo to
liberate the animals. Giraffes will eat telephone pole tops
rhinos bust through World Bank glass tigers devour presidents' leftovers
so no food goes wasted, we all have energy enough to go to space
if we pray we're not there, we have liftoff, soar above Belgrade
and take it with us, the dark blue shreds of its schoolmistress hem
in our hands and claws and beaks. Get out there and whirl on the balcony

before daybreak changes into noon and the colors calm down
becoming pedestrians again crossing the street and cavepainters

probing plums, pointing at the sky digging up worms for sliding
skypictures
                              beaks nearing them with no wings near
no feathers,   plummeting from the daybreak crate
split open by the burning wheel   slices Belgrade open
for twelve hours and sews it up with its disappearance
and leaves a dark violet snailtrail for us to cool under
with apple and construction site and the busted stone clock
on the Paratrooper Club building I will repair when I whirl
on the balcony with the wind electricity and light I generate
I will even ride a giraffe to Mount Avala and burn my head on its peak
so airplanes in fog can see not to slam into me. Grampa Mercy's cough
stopped, rhythm is a distant planet beyond Jupiter it sometimes flickers
in my science fair telescope. I will orbit it only if I can
whirl my way off this balcony and find water in space to baptize
myself Zero Gravity Trombone and blow my way to Rhythm Rhythm
through debris that used to be earth
to ease my dying and live preserved in germless space
close enough to the stars to see if they're really dead--
can a light year be a leap year too? and can I get up and go to the balcony
and cool myself from this coffee spree and listen to the rooster's

rouge tchotchke-box colored cry and die on the vibrating lap of
the varsity soccer captain at Belgrade High.

                              *

three peach pits on the silver balcony railing.
"Zona III" below--"No parking over 180 minutes."
Grampa Mercy coughs in bed, am I keeping him up with my thinking?
Certainly not, what wakes him is compulsive keypunching.
Will I stop? Certainly not. I've just made a fresh cup of
cold white coffee in the beige mug with the blue elephant head handle.
I hold it up by the trunk and sip and feel recharged enough to go
                              till lunch, but then all the letters
will look like cornmush I ate alone too many winters before the TV
watching black and white gangster movies and sipping Jack and
sugar-free caffeine-free Coke with the aspartame in it that
kills my liver, the eagle that plucks me apart as I cry out
strapped to a flickering bluegreen TV screen. three peach pits
on the silvery balcony railing!   bring me back to my self
the mugger with auditory hallucinations of Belgrade Zoo roosters
slycrying through his head where the roadbandit bangs on my eardrums
punctured by a seaside toothpick made from the Adriatic cypress
my favorite sidekick.
                    K, you and I will ride to Athens and
feel sore with sleeping legs by the end of the seventeen hour busride
Godwilling but the landscape will soothe us with its poppypod dusk
and opium open its purple parachute in us as we come become one body
in southern Balkan border checkpoint heat--the crows above Szeged
may be reborn suicides haunting the smugglers calm at baggage check
but I know you and I ride to Athens with smiles and breath enough
to last deep into outer space without oxygen because the Wolfman
from Bug Eyeglow taught us how to deepsea dive by hyperventilating
to drive all the carbon dioxide from our lungs and if we can last
ten seconds longer than we think we can we will gain lightyears of
oxygen and speed through outerspace to meet our kind ancestors
who wait on the dead star for our gift wild strawberry preserves
in glass jars to revive them from celestial slumber and
             rejoin us down here and help us save us humans from auto-
cannibal statehood psychosis, the rogue tower that casts a shadow as cold
as the sarcophagus asleep in the marble quarry.

* * *

confectioner
Dundee cake
across the road

to pack (trunk)
practice
go backwards and forwards

toothbrush
sponge
 sponge-bag

and beach-pyjamas, they're in
nice
to lose one's temper
bathing costume

to shut
tunk trunk
lid
to lock
what a nuisance
travelling-rug

right at the bottom

to unpack
stand up

(voyage--
seaside
seaside place
big luggage
attache case

to miss the train
so much the better
there's no hurry
he didn't want

to look after (somebody)
to enjoy himself
to lock up

mind your backs

careful
to clip
rack

yolk
burst out laughing
a wet afternoon

(my watch is slow
pictures
waterproof

what about you
mending
tapes
to darn

gain
directly
I give it up
cautiousness

I jet with
          language for chats

Po-ro-deesh-te   a threeway mix between nursery theater and family

where maternity ward theater and family meet meet me

convergence excess
and the sheep with the paintball wounds

vacuum cleaner
I'm borne out
to retire

brush up your english
conversations of real use
Hundreds of things.

                              * * *

                          "You are right..."

Gramma Nada tells Grampa Mercy as they argue over who looks like who

"...you don't look like your father or your mother you look like the neighbor.
I'm packed, we're going, help me with these suitcases the sea the mountains
we'll be here a few more days and then bushwhack our way through
the woodsy hills above The Darlings with our silvery machetes
only to find our host family one hour into dinner
too hungry to wait for us and we rudely showing up covered with scars.
They were worried to death we were captured by highway bandits in the cliffs.
Let's go, Mercy, at our age the flesh waits upon no judgement
but car car craves the flora's bluegreen rave

and you are my father Joy after our lunchtime nap and
in the morning yr my husband again and we've got to pack
for the Adriatic then the Wild Boar Mountains
two weeks in each and who cares how long we stay as long as
time is our jumprope we lick salt off in the waves and taste
orange crabshell seconds not that canned crabmeat of home
you keep me sealed in. This tin roof will explode! Give me
the sardine key and turn it with me and let's go speed the serpentines
            to the Adriatic Coast   forget what speedometer reads as we
speedread each other secret recipes and last will and testaments
flashing down the windshield in cinema crawl for the deification of us
speeding in Hitler's yellow folkmachine. You flew a Hunter in the war
hunt down my desire and bring it to me, a beach plate with mudpie
fresh and wet and scented with the fauna of the irradiated sea
the Adriatic bombers dropped gamma cargo leftovers into
so as not to be scolded by commanding officers on deck
on landing on bloodsuds astern."
                          "Nada Nada stop
we're going nowhere we're staying here in our beautiful apartment
in Belgrade sitting on the balcony by the peacelovers blooming
from their pots bright orange and we are in Belgrade so no need to
pack for Belgrade." Mercy calms her.
                          ORIGIN is printed in white letters
down the sides of two of her black wheeled suitcases. She wants to go
                      smiles at the puppetshow on Prince Mercy Street
"Why that's the most delightful thing," the dancing chips beneath their woodsy feet

Does she still wish she could fill jars full of pickled vegetables
for winter closet shelves. She keeps offering me honeydew melon
and Neapolitan chocolates and saying "I want to eat more but you'll
call me greedy. I am your Nana, you are my firstborn, I raised you,
did everything but breastfeed you you loved me more than your mother--
                                              need I say more?

                    Silence is better!
You are not my husband Mercy you are my father Joy and I am your daughter
Nada Seadweller. We escaped civil war by dumb luck, a fluke when Freedom
could have ordered his men to shoot. Our people were ready in the national
bank with Kalashnikovs loaded. Why don't you want more honeydew melon?
You're full? When did you eat? Do you have a woman? Where are those women
who slept on the couch last night? If you ever see your date waiting for you
at the fountain's edge with a closed umbrella in his hand and it's not even
raining, flee the city--New York Belgrade or Trieste--let's go to the beach
and make mudpies to feed the starving children packed
in transfer cases wrapped in flags. Let's pack and reminisce how
my brother Dear Owleye worked Alexanderplatz blackmarket after the war

and returned home with enough stories to lull us to sleep a million nights.
How he made us walk his shoes and in return made us halvah
we loved as chocolate was scarce during the war and called a truckload
of cabbage delivered to our cranky older sister Buca's and
left a message for her to call the zoo for Bojana who turned out to be a
bear. Nada's heart, eat one more honeydew melon wedge for Nada's love.
Do you hear how Nada's boylet has not a trace of accent
as if he lived all his life in Belgrade. That's my influence--
                                        Flipped Baba!"

                            *

I want to lap myself
in my race against me
come home and throw no homecoming party
get right to the work of
everyday Oming practicing

breathing through a straw, spinning, looking at red needles
seeing the common nothing in all the phobia objects
you avoid. Embrace them and they are shelled

not like an attacked city
but like a crab you have to eat to survive
on the wild isle mind, the biggest killer
in the whirligig nightlife Adriatic coast
a few years ago you couldn't see a shooting star for all the cannon fire
from boats and cliff fortresses.

I want to lay down my race baton
part with my relay team

"I'm packed
four wheeled suitcases by the front door
for the sea the mountains Belgrade
for my return to young flesh

I will walk to my parents' home and kiss my father
who will not turn back into my husband
in the morning when I pack and make salad sandwiches for the trip
to the coast"

            oh fuck it no more talking wounds

                                        shut your mouth and sleep
piss this white coffee out whirling on the terrace

the seahorse is held together with glue and you're using yours up
with the temperature you thrive at

and spill white coffee out of your mug on the balcony
and breathe for three peach pits on the silvery balcony railing
and listen to sink pipes above play tunes for you and neighbors
waking up for work while you steady yourself for bed
intoning the word ALLUVIALS and
drawing your attention to breakfast
missing the present and
                    its pink oil-on-canvas ass

                    Wolfman says you're a masochist

I am the heaven of the castrated children of the cannibal revolution
the last choirboy to leave practice with priest's scalp in one hand
and Alka-Seltzer tablets to sub for communion wafers in the other
when I rouse me in my fields of mass.

I am the ozoneless earth. Where did you hide my rind? My pulp rots in
      space.

7/21/05
Beograd, Srbija i Crna Gora
Belgrade, Serbia and Montenegro

PART 2: BELA KAFA

mixing it you may grow to like it

                                 white coffee.
in all my years as a monarch
        I've never seen such enthusiasm over a beverage
              except absinthe when
                            THE END

*

dear K,
       tonight
at Republic Square

Your voice is   the green on the Paratrooper Club's broken
       clock
weathered longtime color.

K's smile is light green oxygen.

...

tonight I heard in my nap:
where blood can find me
find me
and where you can dine on my body
the blood speaks complete sentences in my ears.

here blood speaks complete sentences in my ears.

Belgrade Sentence

Blood speaks complete sentences in my ears.

        the blood loaches in my ears.

conversations of real use (cont.)

to listen in
occasionally

to switch on to
knowledge

peace and quiet
4-valve
atmospherics

to sling ink
            off-hand
                    dispatche
  quill-driver

scald
    disjecta

Blueballs
is what I have, Sis,
from looking at you.
I know it's a sin to commit incest
but to admit it's a desire
how do you feel about that?
I will never ask you
unless we're drunk one night in
a Chalkidiki beach bar on
a stolen light blue jug of ouzo

and I try to kiss you and you
break the jug on the table and cut my jugular.

That would be okay since the last person I'd see would be you.

       Balkan blueballs
"Sram ti ushao i nikad izashao," said Iva to me when I was leaving as the
pool-party crowd came--"Shame came into you and never left."
I would ever even want to have sex with you

unnattainable   favorite subject   focus
    Belgrade
                             Laughter

"For all your ills I give you..."
                     tonight
         a hot bath
       the last
             things around you start again.

        *

Nada:
"I broke up with my highschool love. It doesn't matter who kicked who.
I rode my bike down a hill too fast--
crashed, was in a cast from the waist down
in the hospital for the liberation of Belgrade in '44
the bombs the shells...an artillery shell hit right above my head
and blew a big hole in the wall behind my hospital bed--
missed me by about a foot--my head. But let's not talk of ugly things--"

    --Had it not missed you none of us would be

         everybody makes their own

          forehead crammed with creases

                    prime sunlight hours
even if it's moderately overcast you will get the light you need.
Grandfather reads the obituaries by lamplight in his living room.

          Who were the exstatics today?

salamander on Kalemegdan fortress bricks, Roman Well, recall--

Her four black wheeled suitcases packed--where's she going?

"We'll be here a few more days, then we're going to the sea or the mountains or..."

I wish to praise her. She's sick and I'm using her for my muse.
   Is this sick of me? True Muse, please DO sing in me

that I may stop using other people for their language
their strange Belgrade speech. Silence.

What's there to eat? Belgrade air and plum knoedl and
cream pie. In Belgradesugarhigh I wonder how the dinosaurs

traveled before the meteor ended their travels--
who have I not seen here yet of relatives and how offended are they

and what meteors will end this version of earth
civilization way out of date, obsolete humans on space rock.

Her four black wheeled suitcases packed--
                              She's in Belgrade, going to
                                      Belgrade

         after her afternoon nap.

                              cleaned up for tourists

                    The Roman Well in Belgrade's Kalemegdan fortress
                    made by Austrians.

LICENSE TO WALK (WOLFMAN'S SOLO)

after twelve years in Belgrade I have a license to walk
--my passport--
Ladies and Gentlemen!
I can walk! It was not Christ--
I did not go down to the river
to be washed for walking--
I did not walk from a case against me--
Rather--my papers are in order! Before the cops
would stop me and ask for my ID and haunt me

"What kind of ID is this?"
"A refugee ID"
"Give me a break--where did you get this--c'mon
we'll go easy on you--"
They couldn't arrest me--they knew full well
an ID it was. But if they had the time
they could torture me as long as they liked--
and they liked--boy did they like!

Now that I have my passport in my pocket
sometimes I touch its soft blue cover and pages
virginal, without one stamp--
after twelve years
in Belgrade,   fleeing the burning school in my Bosnian
hilltop town in a bus envisioning how I would
end myself with the gun in my backpack...

WHAT THE WOLFMAN SAID

I feel good in advance about these washing machines.
      What's in them? Come see !
           boats on high seas, pirates, an arrow through a pirate gun
I'm ready for a gallery solo exhibition
        and to live in a tent for the next twelve years
            so I can keep
      painting! What is painting to me?
              Let me tell you the things
               in my washing machine:
the voices I hear in my washing machine as I paint them...

7/23/05

40

AT DARA'S BIRTHDAY PARTY

We must go into the grave business.
Business never goes bad for death.

                              Tonight
I disrobed to pack a suitcase
and drag it to the door to go   above the jet

          fades: you can see it from the terrace after a night
of breaking away from the party for a spell to look out over

                         Belgrade lights--
is this a metropolis now that I've arrived?

We must go into the grave business

                         shave the barnacles off each other's faces and
emerge refreshed to face the smashed plaster chips
                         on the way to Baba Nada's.

Enter and four black wheeled packed suitcases still stand against
the brown polished china cabinet--   three pink candles lit
               on the dining table and seven candlebulbs
     above the chandelier--

                    can it fry me? And will you salt me well before
you fillet me, you locals who can take this bombardment and converse on
enduring shrapnel months

                    --we're going into the grave business
and will accept as wedding gifts only call-bells you
will be able to hear "above ground sucking air" in your furnished

                    faces--white stubble--packedeyebags--yes age is
eyeduct luggage lost in the shade's airplane--each new wrinkle
a freshly dug trench--

```
FLUTE-SPINE!
Summer thinks
I abandoned her
for a cave
with a typewriter
and enough John Patmos gas
to get me high enough
to sing Jazz Mass at
```

THE READING

            concerned with the reader
                                       ship.
                topic. A soap sliver disappears while you shower
can you bathe while Nada sleeps, the running water might impede
her attempts at catching wet dream centipede. Could you please pass
the silver, what gift is for whom. See with your ears
smell with your tongue you fish with rearranged organs
each line is a gill you grow to breathe in underwater western world
with seaweed dangling from your mouth and flying like a lone
yellow party streamer in a fan.

                  "A smile refreshes the mind--"

       Summer thinks I abandoned her for the voices in my head,
nonsense, I told Dawn I said I didn't pinch my words
"Pinch my golden ashcake self into your rollup cig when I'm noth but
spectral id I'll get you high one last time." Did she? She did?

                    ...

dark blue packed suitcases not black
dammit poet work with the lights on

hire yourself at least once a day
the sun burns on by celebrating itself

                    ...

Nada sings at the kitchen table:

        IDE MILE I TARABE BROJI
        IZASHLA BIH AL NESMEM OD SVOJIH!

        [THERE GOES MEELEH AND HE COUNTS THE FENCES
        I'D GO OUT BUT CAN'T 'CUZ OF MY PARENTS!]

                    ...

Grampa Mercy reads obituaries again tonight in lamplight

        spitting out green flesh of too green plums.

                    ...

    muse   (please do it
               sing in me

            and through me tell the story of Popeye and the Sirens
            Cali and mountain lions
            Palatine Humidor and Environs

            oh but to find things where they be--
            Muse do please assist me--
            you flicker in Mark's lightblue email screen and
            the quiet things he types me--(--

            "Muse, hah? Sounds progressive!"

                    * * *

life can be
          might as well
                    when things are

I. green simpletons chanting at beehives for sneakers, 2. breathe, III.
      awful good better best sightseeingly lightning boltish and
      like that prom went swimmingly dingdong bell
      my nurse became a date who blew me in a snowheap outside the
      aviary--

"Mark, I'm in Belgrade getting the seat
cushion hot before the keys and kneeling to ask Her
for Dictation, Assistance, Eggwhites."

                              "Whoa--sounds progressive!"

                    *

                              rather than a social register

  I've noticed
          rag   bout   vacation

I really do have those scars
                    rags
                    art
                         ...that bar topic?
(navy blue suitcases of Nada still stand by china cupboard and
      blonde wheat spears in a blue and white porcelain pitcher above)

                    like showing off...
                         it's only
                              protection

                                        *

                         what stocking
               did you hang yourself with
               or was that a comet you reached for
               and fell off the terrace or
                    was it getting up out of the beach chair
          from Stone Beach white wine drunk
               as your sister came up and asked
          "What yr up here alone watching Belgrade City Lights?"

            among cinema floodlights
                popcorn galaxy
                                        black carpet ant ministry
        usher glasses
                    dropped between red cushioned seats

        rats rustling in popcorn bags
in back of you

                                    a call bell
            the bellhop rings
                            demanding service
        from bespectacled clientele shaking in their suites!

I think of your Belgrade as a different social notation

I guess the rest of the day like a gossip will die eventually
          its belly will burst in the grave
                    all its feast day meals will erupt
                    rendering the corpse in twain
               twain--something volcano like!
          igneous bubblings will dictate
          the hairline ideology of death

                                        fre e dom now
                                        rest when ash

--Ah, but Sir...your golden ashcake ate us
when we tried to break it apart...

               --In that case let me help you
                    here is my icecream moustache
                         lick it and see the stars at twenty
          then watch them age and die like you and still send light

          Grampa Mercy's newspaper Belgrade trembles in his hands
                         by lamp with golden stem and off white shade
                    with light green rim...

                              ***

--I am yr brother, Natalie, why do you scream at me?

     --She doesn't remember you.

          --Who is this kid who comes around every other summer
          writes down what everybody says at parties and
               then disappears and never publishes
                    our conversations. Thief! if he gives not
                    to us freely if he escapes to Greece
                         to be with boys half his age and play
                         lost tourist blissy mister
                         with them--we will dismember him
                         and deposit his fragments
                         in ATM slots
                              and when the banker sees them he'll
                              cough and work on
                                   but we'll be peacefuller than before
          and looking at the lion's head in her arms
                    our mother will say "Hey--that's my son
                    --how a face changes!"

                    ...

notation
make it your home

social
page
save
compose

check your head at cUStoms
when you enter US

pick it up before you flee
to Belgrade--white city--

comb your hair in a callbell
and wait for the poolside starter pistol.

munchen scene on an antique beermug

church steeple and dark blue dusk
    green bushes and inside

                star parts are my business and
      used star lots
          I am that greased up salesman of the

      shoreline--
why all things are portable in this age of rope.

          come down off that balcony
Belgrade lights are down here in the living room too
 not just out there over the Starry Aria Hills
   and today Dara is five!

I am stuck in a dark blue blouse pocket of the sky like a forgotten vitamin--
take me! or I melt and stain your rising falling lipstick-marked
       chest--Treasure
with your pirate gaptooth grin

                  *

having destroyed the view of oneself as really existing

      will US know it's war until we have to use rations?

  ...

Grampa gets up from the newspapers and--bent over--
      trips toward the bathroom--
  --What's happening?
  --I lost myself in reading ...

*

callbellgrade

      *

I am landlocked
painting four stories
moved to D-- W-- Street
I. Diamond Wallabee   2. Dieter Willing   III. Dialed Wig
to get laid like ink.
The Roman Well in Belgrade's Kalemegdan Fortress was made by Austrians.

     *

```
creature of / of a team with wings
of the lovely step here beside us
like the roof tops
:; yet I would also swing
to the running of the trace-horse. *
                                *

                                                    *

            *
                                                          *
                *
                                                    *


                P*L*E*I*A*D*E*S

...


                                replaced your esophagus


                        in Asheville

                                    Love,
                                        a piping plover
                                        a typing poet
                                        a crooked trail of bells
                    P.S. reply
                            move
                                guide
        check your tongue between my musethighs and die
            ,my Verse
                        like the Brazillian electrician 27
                    in London 5 rounds in him
                            the planet rounds the sun
                            how long till it
                                    flicks us off its back
                rodeo clown space will not save US from broncometeorwhitehooves
        the brown saddle browner with dried blood of the rUSset
                    mantle clad in dewdawn kindly on off with self head

                    I am thy father's lyric
                    doomed for a certain time to feed you lines
                     when you dry and corpse and fly on wires
                     above my white prompter robe
```

in my box the script is eaten by ringworms starved for humans
                    ready to take over Earth and give it rings like Saturn
                bite by bite

almighty dear spirit Virginia
yes there is a Belgrade
punch your callbell ring and see
the sixth sense is a threnody you hear in the shower
and a mourning dove goochaying in dawn sky opening like a firstgrader's
                    first bright blue plastic pencil case ...

*

                            A writes:
"I'm done with my Che biography though I dream of being in his army
sometimes." Funny, I was just in La Revolucion last night with
    the red bettertimesBelgrade icon of Che as backdrop for us drinkers
    a photo of Subcommandante Marcos or one of his million doubles
        in black skimask and smoking wooden pipe
  and three ladies blonde in white matching uniform
            came up to Wolfman and me and offered us red or light Winstons
            "Are you a smoker Sir?" Wolfman puffed it for three drags
    and said "Too perfumed Filly I never put out cigarettes till filter"

and he put it out in front of the red Che icon
"Comrades and Comradets"
it says on W.C. doors
if only communism could save us from death's velvet kitchen
I'd sign up tonight

                        --What night friend? Permanuclear sun bleaches us
                        in the washing machine planet we spin in
                            fabric softener moustache
                                what girl will kiss that
                                if in space there are girls
            dial their mobiles
                            my mobile twirls above my crib I disappear
            waving into the garbage truck before my driveway
            I'm going to the sea and mountain like Nada
                my baba I keep up   key-punching
                    Munchen the church steeple the dark blue dusk
                with red roof
                                what rebels hide in those mountains?
        A and Che kiss in a hammock stretched between two cavemouths
                                                    and sing
            selfmade moodmusic echoes
                                back from the stone palate
                                rocky epiglottis
                        if the bats enter
                            there's a chance
                        oxygen remains on the oilrigraped planet--

and water? no trace--the trace-horse a flyfeast
                                            his rider
                        disappeared by vulture hygeine ring...

                                        .
                                         .
                                     .   . .
                            ----******----*)(-----
                                     .
                                     .
                                      .
                                       .
                                    Help

                    *

                        "a blast of hello in the midst of
                            this dark distance"
                                    writes A
                dear Sister Distance

                        I pray for you
             your safe travels and skin-stretching birth

        *

    a catscream and the dashboards blinking blue
         Convergence Excess, have at you
                I put on my reading glasses ...

                                    *

    what did I not notice? the laundry line smell
                  damp and green
                      where were the flying sisters this dawning?
         who says they weren't flying there?   peace to them--
signed, The Pilot Light
                   Alles Liebe
                        Jonnie

                              . . .

each dot of the threedot ellipses is the father the son the holy spirit

Sister Ellipses pray for me that what I come up with after you is peaceful
        enough to be true
and not some crazy fancy I cramp my way up to
          like most of this nightraving poetry seems to tend to
as I use my tendons to do it do I do it who else do it but me here alone
      who do I talk to? A? Wolfman? Rockefeller?
Who still coughs deep inside Kaukas rock and screams as bald eagle
              picks his liver apart and drops the pieces on
                      a war-room gameboard
      STOP . . .

*

                                breathe and roll
              love yourself or
                                    down down down you go
          alone   not a callbell to comb your hair in
                          pomegranate seeds pierce yr skin silent
      death gives you a tetanus shot in the eyelid
      welcoming you to burning galleys

blow those pink candles out before your attempt at atmosphere
        blows you into space with this gas coming in now what am I
              in Patmos cave? no only Cereno Belgrade Place
                  a sunburned mutineer on the vine-busted deck
                  what you did before determines
                    whether you go overboard a dolphin
                      fleeing spotted panthers
                          lynxes dangling from crow's nest
                  hyenas loafing on messhall scraps
                    your scrappaper face torn by a cry
                        for air and awake breath as you
                    steer GrapePurplePrince D
                    to Naxos Home Island
                        where Ariadne waits to walk with him
                          off the cliff and become
                              a new tune in the oxygen mix--

```
      I'm totally uninterested in the sewer system am I?
a good way to end up in it!

heart palpitations, go away
                    I'm having Art Palpitations
              I must stay
                      in Belgrade morning ink
           until I'm sane
                        enough to kiss the living room windowpane
                              Goodmorning .
```

RT 4: BALKANSKA GRAFOMANIA
NA BEOGRADSKIM ULICAMA
BALKAN GRAPHOMANIA
ON BELGRADE STREETS

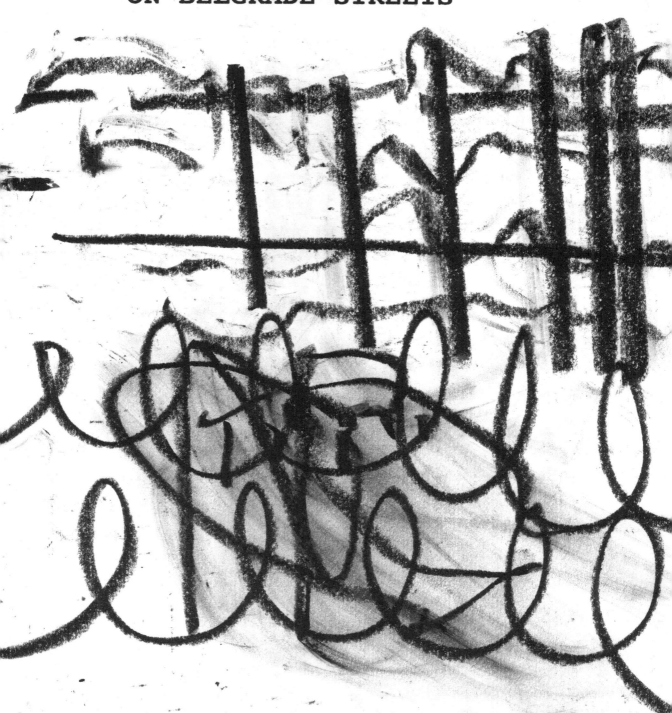

QUOTATIONS FROM IRRADIATED BELGRADE

                              yr mother in '91
on the eve of Balkan

              orange

              quotations

My English
 is not very goodnik!

          (steel beams--lines
            skyscraper times
                Babel Towers sliced
limes for cocktail Oceanside--)

. . .

Grampa Mercy on Che--
"He was a real revolutionary
because he got rule,
gave up all the privileges of rule,
and went to Bolivia to
raise a revolt with the Indians."

2.

You like Belgrade?
You like the inspiration
you receive here
among family--million cousins--?

Befriend radiation--
deal with traces of
depleted uranium bombing
by NATO in '99

while you were demonstrating
they were detonating--!
            Think you can
come here and make your
poems for free? Stop thinking!

You can take a little
depleted uranium cell-killer
with you--fatal souvenir
you may find blooming in you

tomorrow or in 2 or 20 years!

who is there to protect you? Nobody.
Enjoy Belgrade. And when you get home
send me a postcard from Indian Point.
          Toothless on bombed slopes of Parnassus,
                                     your muse,
                                          Liberty

3.

Belgrade Evening Radiation Haze
     on Revolution Boulevard--
     Nope!
 King Aleksandar Boulevard--and Street of the
Proletariat Brigades--now Crown Street
again--name changes--
          radiation staynges--
          _____

human remains--
       ruins--
          knaves--
     knives--
   plays--

in the dead con's maze
       the predators rave

$.4.

Machine
Time
Washing
Machine
  Time can't be washed
     in our lifetime
      we have to die

 Proudly say We
 amidst the jeers
  of the audience
      and scream
     to be financed
          by everybody present

               For Poetry!

```
                    letters
        mints    glass    tumbling
        in white washing machine
                                hissing!


5.

        LIVE CANTOS OPEN ALL NIGHT // ALIVE IN THE BELGRADE AFTERLIFE //
            VIVA CONCEPTION!


6.

Filipe, ajd me poljubi
I daydream her saying
my loins go hot
the lineaments of
I want her--

In her red and white
checkered dress tonight
LEGS--Bowlegged walk--
WOW--(Pause) (Pause)

who? who?
          hurts your cock
blueballs on Balkan Boy

and what line! in     her walk--
a dance on Prince Mihajlova Street
Ajd me poljubi, Filipe   Da Da Da


7.

I     as we sat at Republic Square
eating pizza
              nearly spontaeneously
turned to kiss her
     surrounded          by
       strolling seated walking
                 LOVERS!

"When we two parted" she didn't press
            her breast to mine--
              got in the cab w/ a smile--
```

8.

I belong to K--

        * * *

Should I wear a lead apron
        on the busride
                        to Greece?

Aunt Ivana says :
                Since the '99 bombing
                        the cancer rate jumped 32 percent.
                                Milosevic told us
                                it was uranium but
                        we didn't believe him we thought
        America's a civilized country, they wouldn't
                they did
                        millions of NATO soldiers at Kosovo
                                        radiation sick to death
                                        Belgrade too
                depleted uranium rain

*

                                                on the flight deck
                excessive heat warnings

                                        "It does feel different
                        I supposed we feel a bit unsafe" [London 2005 July]
the body parts [that were] propelled into the trees

                                                        were removed

                        by cherry pickers--

*

DON'T STEER

                    listen
                         breathe
                              quilldriver
                                        drive on
                    through block radiation nugget

TYPEWRITER FORTRESS--A TYPEWRITER PORTRAIT OF GRAMPA MERCY

1. WHAT'S YOUR FAVORITE ISLAND?

--Mljet is my favorite island
        an island near Dubrovnik
completely covered with forest
    in the center a lake of sea water
        flows through a very slim
                        a narrow canal.

My favorite color is Adriatic blue--
        nothing better than flying over the blue Adriatic--
like a flying free bird--
without any control--
totally alone--.

--Tell me all the memories you have of Mljet.

--In the center of the lake there is an island and on it a hotel
but I was not in it
but I lived in a tent
and I enjoyed the island there was sand on it--
and I enjoyed a well-prepared fish
the natives of Mljet caught in the lake--
a saltwater lake in the middle of Mljet Island--

anyway Mljet is known
                    famous--for it is full of mongooses--
who multiplied since the government brought them in from Indonesia
a non-indigenous life form
imported to destroy the snakes
various snakes--

When the snakes disappeared the mongooses started to feed on
chicks and chickens and other farmlife
of the natives.

They--in this way they changed from do-gooders to damagers--

2. WHO WAS YOUR FIRST LOVE?

--I was watching in the theater a production from Hunterville
and I looked around at the audience through opera glasses.
When the production finished
one of my aquaintances
brought her friend
to meet me. I never knew such

                              one girl
who liked me instantly
that is how my first love began

                    (GRAMMA NADA ENTERS)

--Where is my mother?

--She's dead.

--Don't say things like that, Tata.
Where is Mother?
In the pantaloons pocket is stuck green powder detergent
 to clean our teeth.
   It is four-thirty time for Sister Milena to come over.

--Sister Milena's not coming, Nada.

--Why? Oh yes. She has to teach a class today.

--The love affair lasted short
everything lasted only one spring and one summer.

--Don't talk like that Tata
don't dirty your pants or lose your glasses
later you will suck the blood from our veins for it.
Does my Tata want coffee--

--One spring and summer lasted, right?
Because in the city arrived a foreigner a stranac a stranger who
        yanked away my first love--

...

I was fifteen--it was to me fifteen years--

I had fifteen years--

...

                                  a slightly older stranger

...

took her away from me--my first love--Ana--

...

3. WHAT WERE YOUR FIRST IMPRESSIONS OF THE US?

--First of all--when we arrived in Miami Beach--comma--
  I was splashed by the richness of the hotels and
        the beauty of the nature--
but very quickly I learned two things
  that Americans are individually good people--BUT
        that for them--now open the parenthesis--I mean the quotes

              "That the dollar is your master
                  and you may not have other gods
                        besides him"--

(Nada comes in to hang her wet freshly washed dress on the balcony
laundry line)

--Sister Milena--where did she run off to?   (PAUSE)
        See how your Grampa gives you company
              remember that when we die--

        ***

--At once I eyed
the ugly--in Miami beach--
ugly appearance--apparition--
segregation and exploitation of position of blacks--
as they were then called by progressives--
including the violence over them--

--I was enchanted by
the tall productivity of working people

              who worked hard so they could support the front
          against the Japanese and Germans
                protiv sila osovine--against the Axis powers--
        against the Tripartite Pact--

I was   --say: I was enchanted by the patriotism and
          the tall productivity of the people--
  like the beauties of the American pejsaze [landscapes] --
        Dosta? [Enough?]

        --No.

...

4. WAS THERE PANIC AT THE BEGINNING OF W.W. II?

                                        --There was no panic
there was worry over the soldiers on the front.

          If you speak of landscapes there you may say
          from the Niagara waterfalls
                    to the Arizona desert
               and Monterey Bay in California--
               I'm saying when I told you about the landscapes
                    insert that.

                              The most popular song at that time
     was WHITE CHRISTMAS
                         because it expressed the...

--Desire?

--It's not desire   LONGINGS of the
                         soldier

     for his home and God's budding flowers and festivities.
Besides the classical dances there appeared the BOOGIE WOOGIE
about which till then I'd not known--

--How was it danced?

               --Like it is danced now, don't you know--
the predecessor of rock n' roll--
                         which I never learned--
because I opposed it with the Viennese Waltz and the Argentine Tango.
One girl tried to teach me but I didn't want to--
a Jewish girl you can say.

--Did you ever try to learn the BOOGIE WOOGIE?

                         (He taps his thick reading glasses
                         against the white and brown kitchen
                         table
          with its tablecloth of brown and white flowers)

                                        --There was a balance
        I was preparing for war
                            for Air Force--and along with that
        I used my free time to aquaint myself with people and land

        and I created many friends.

You can add this: Then we Serbs were very popular--
                as Chetniks (the King's guerilla army)
                    u Americi--in America--

                            --Was socialism ever in view?

  --By my thinking New Deal was a road out of Great Depression--
  and in that way to save the existing order--

which allowed America to employ its capacities
            and squiggle around the crisis--

period.
After Pearl Harbor
the state was taking total control over the economy--
which always brought out a quicker exit from crisis and
a more prosperous support of the front--of wartime idealisms--
at the same time protecting ekonomija in balance.

--If you were holding a talk to the soldiers in Baghdad what would you say?

--That that which they are doing is not good for themselves, for America
        and for the world (period).
instead of helping the world poor
                            and in that way creating friends for
                                            themselves.

                America is--America started out
            on the road
                    of an imperial power--and is coming upon

                the resistance of the subjugated--

        who have no other exit than terrorism
            and it is the only vehichle with which the downtrodden
                worker
                    can resist the powerful.

--What would you tell the young in America's cities about resistance?

--To fight for one better America--less militant--and more good-creating
        good-acting--and in this way create a better life for
            themselves

and for the rest of the world--instead of a hundred millions
        for arming--to ask   that big means   be used for the good
      and not the destruction of people--the destruction of life.

Dosta?

--Yes--

    (He shrugs his shoulders and looks at me.)

    --I don't know what else I'd say,
       enough it is   that which I said.

Maybe I could say
                 something: (taps glasses on table)
        To battle against the Cocacolazation and Hollywoodization
 of the culture   comma and for the real culture's value.

5. WHAT WAS THE FIRST IMAGE YOU REMEMBER?

                       The first image I saw in my life
   was the First World War, at the end of the First World War
     when the soldiers who escaped from the front
       and came returned home

                  burned the Austro-Hungarian empire flag--

--Do you know that it is the anniversary of the start of the first World War?

--Yes soon it will be the Second World War
       wars always begin in autumn, or in the spring--

```
--Why do they begin in spring?

      --In spring so they're finished by fall--

                 and in the fall because the harvest is gathered
                        to get through the war winter
          for the leading of an as-short-as-possible war.

    Instead of "in the autumn" you should say "end of summer"--you know--
                    that change--


...

In modern times the history shows not one war was short.
In modern times.
Not the First not the Second not Iraq--

                                     even the one against Yugoslavia
      lasted longer than they hoped
                                which was begun illegally
          without the okay of the United Nations
    against Yugoslavia.

                      The moment the European Union took the role of
        mediator in the internal conflicts in Yugoslavia--
                    that was the biggest mistake
                  Yugoslavia made--that it allowed
                    the mixing of outsiders into its internal
                          workings
                  (period).  because mediators didn't serve Yugo
            slavia but their own interests:
     "Germany before everything" so as to liquidate
                    the results of the First and Second war of the
                    Balkans--

                      before everything say: Germany
          in the continuation of imperial doctrine Drang Nach Osten
            "penetration into the East"--
          and with this they tried to nullify the results of
          the First and Second World Wars on the Balkans.

My first memory is--the soldiers returning from the First World War
to Bugojno, Bosna lit the flag of the AustroHungarian empire on fire
in front of my home. I had then four years.
```

--What just fell on my smartness
on my mind?
In the global cell no one is sure...
in the global village no one can be sure or secure--
or independent--

but you should add:
                    as long as force is
                                    the way of solving world problems
no one can be sure in the global cell

no one can be secure in the global cell

as long as power is the way of solving the world's problems
            from one side or another
                    no one can be secure in the global cell.

Belgrade, Serbia and Montenegro
July 2005

BOOK II:

ZERO READERSHIP

...

BEOGRADSKI DRUM

BELGRADE ROAD

6/28/06 - 7/9/06
Belgrade, Serbia

L
A
U
N
C
H
P
A
PART 1: DICTIONARY

EXTENDED FAMILY VOICES 2

1. NURSE MIRA OVERHEARS

> GRAMMA NADA AND GRAMPA MERCY SITTING AT THE
> KITCHEN TABLE AS NADA, COMING OUT OF A TRANCE,
> BEGINS TO CRY:

--Mercy...what is this that's happening to us?

> PAUSE

--Darling, you...are sometimes forgetting things.

> PAUSE

--Aha...why are we not with our children in America?

> SILENCE

--Because nobody wants us there.

> GRAMPA MERCY BEGINS TO WEEP.

2. TELEPHONE YELL

Grampa Chaki called me today while I was eating lunch at Grampa Mercy's apartment:

> --DID YOU TAKE DOWN MY TWO PICTURES OF MILOSEVIC?

--YES.

--WHERE DID YOU PUT THEM?

--INTO THE DRAWER UNDER YOUR BOWL OF PIPES. I DIDN'T WANT HIM LOOKING AT ME WHILE I SLEPT, ESPECIALLY TWO OF HIM.

--LISTEN DON'T YOU MESS WITH ME!!! I AM A SICK MAN! ! ! YOU PUT THEM BACK, YOU HEAR ME? I'M GOING TO CALL SOME PEOPLE AND HAVE THEM TALK TO YOU! I LIKE VERY MUCH TO BE A GOOD GRAMPA AND YOU A GOOD GRANDSON BUT
THIS REALLY HAS NO SENSE!

--GOOD. OKAY.

> He hung up.

3. BELGRADE DETAIL

From the basement of Plato's internet cafe
I write you, Dear Alien Mantaray,

SPACE IS TRIP
AND LAND IS SHIP
FOR BOMBS TO RIP
AND HANDS TO HIT
    BODY IN FITS
    NERVES IN BITS
    LAUGHTER LIFTS
    QUICKLIME TO LIPS
NO OTHER'S HANDS TO KISS

    . . .

IN A CIRCLE
        Nada's nurse Mira mutters to herself
                            IN A CIRCLE
                                    above
                   a map of the newly divided
             Serbia , Croatia , Bosnia
Dear Alien,
        when I looked into my brand new red and blue
       pocket dictionary the first word I found was
        CRANKSHAFT

    I had hallucinations.

--Auditory or visual?

--Both. In stereo.

    . . .

Teenage boys playing video games beside me
Talk and I will translate them with liberty:

"I will die yesterday."

"Good, I don't have that kind of time."

"You're daylosing."

"Not daylosing. Playing a videogame
in Plato's basement internet cafe
in Belgrade tobacco cloud THUNDERCRACK

in uranium mine mining my very self
making bombs to blow you to pixels!"

4. STUDENT INTERLUDE

Education rips up your wizard sleeves

You travel to weave new ones

Travel makes you a robe of
feathers of cemetery geese
of Brooklyn where you walked
past graves with Julien and Kailey
last June before you came to Belgrade Ecstasy.

5. MARRIAGE ADVICE FROM MERCY

"A man has to get married, otherwise
in four walls alone he dies dies dies..."

Mercy echoes in my basement moment tobacco head.

The videogame boys keep talking but
new material is not forthcoming.

When you listen for the overheard note
it never comes. Stop listening and into
the typing it comes. Typing is TRACTION
when you slide on wet night road mind.

5.5 MARRIAGE ADVICE FROM MERCY 2

"A man has to get married, otherwise
in four walls alone / he's a suicide..."

Mercy echoes in

                    girls and boys
                                    coming.

6. AUNT IVANA AND NURSE MIRA:

The NATO planes came for three months. Spring of '99. Left trauma traces
on many people.

                BLACK NIGHT NOT A LIGHT ON--
                Then--FLASH--

                sometimes they just circle
                all night for three hours and
                don't drop a single bomb
                and you're like HIT ME ALREADY!

    ...

A schoolteacher was catching
empty air on a streetcorner.
When people asked her
"What are you doing, Miss?"
she said

      "CATCHING AIRPLANES"

    ...

In Vojvodina they bombed they hit it they spanked it
hard the cornfields they hit every day and in Belgrade
the AJAXES passed over filming everything low filming
the hospitals schools and Generalshtab headquarters to
hit and the television building to hit most of the
targets were civilian targets PREMEDITATED
COLLATERALDAMAGE.

                                (Basement boys play video
                                games in tobacco smoke.
                                  "The grip is ours, Fool! Throw
                                  something! Why did you stop?")

The Serbs made tanks out of wood and the Americans
bombed the hell out of the wooden tanks but the uranium went
into the ground it will leave in 7,000 years don't worry
nobody reports about that but history and statistics will show
what happened. The planes bombed funerals in progress,
hospitals full of civillians, cornfields in Vojvodina

where farmers had to go in groups to pick the harvest
or starve--the bombs took them all.

The cancer rates in the sanitariums for consumptive
people in the mountains are rising fast. Once
ecological paradises, now birthing places for
two-headed children. An experiment in radioactive
warfare. Belgrade was hit too, not as hard, but they
rocked it, with depleted uranium bombs, usually used
only against tanks, but with all that surplus, what's
to lose.

        (SURPL-US-AURUS, EXTINCT EMPIRE,

                            alive at your own wake,
                            Zombiehood

        ****

        Wolfman
        Are you making her cucumber
        finger sandwiches? Always
        be making the Muse
        cucumber finger sandwiches
        or she will make cucumber finger sandwiches
        of you!)

        ****

The bombings changed the weather.
I've never seen it this humid till after.

                        The only time I've
felt this humidity is New York.   when I came back here
after the bombing, the summers changed

                            They set
us up good. And we've always been best at knockin'
'em down. Coffee?

7. STUDENT INTERLUDE 2

                         Despite the uranium
                           in our food and water
                         we are happier here
                            in Belgrade
                           than all of you in America
                         with all your conveniences--
                           dying a death by surplus--
                           A HEAP OF
                                 SURPLUS GOODS
                           BURYING YOU
                             and your senses--

ELEGY DIARY

No one dead yet today
that I know. If they died
would I have the where-
withal to write them an elegy
immediately--
Let's see. Pretend somebody died! I can'
T. No pretending. Back to work, what are
you doing here do you know how many emails you have to answer--
emails of the dead! Writing you from their text pads
on the coffin lid while they're out for a death smoothie
with lots of wheatgrass in it which decreases concentration.
Meanwhile in Troy I breaking Hektor, breaker of horses
I Achilles with this sharp toothbrush stuck in my heel beg your mercy
O Gods, for all the poems I Accept are for you and therefore
to you I return them, written in wet crayon on my bleeding heel--
take them and me away from all this breath because I never
learned breathing properly otherwise I would have stayed home and
pretended to be a husband or gone in drag to wash laundry
so the Gods wouldn't come draft me. Oh Gods,
that's you again, no escaping what's closer to you than the
veins in your neck. Heck, I'
d like to call you all for dinner, Gods, and read my hymns of praise
to you which you dictated to me in my waking stages between infancy
and puberty, when I was only 9 years old in the mushroom cult steambath
composing the threnody to last, and we ought to linger long enough
at the supermarket shelf to see ourselves in bags of poisonous
spinach. I'm spinning from something, must be the placebo God I just
swallowed, must be the mountain I climbed down slow so
my bloodcells would settle down and the blood must be the blood
bubbles not forming in my blood because I'm surfacing slow enough
from the depressiocean depths to speak to you, Dr. Phillips,
of the traumas endured and the traums still traum'd and
the trams taken through Belgrade during the war when tramrides were free
and on bombing days Republic Square was full for rock concerts
and no school and everybody went to the theater free and everything
was free because of the threat of imminent NATO bombdeath and
Zorana stayed up doing her math homework anyway by tomahawk green light
        flashes
in her window and learned algebra in dust swinging up from
Belgrade concrete, which is a curious furious mixture of blood, bombs,
and human feet.

BEOGRADJANKA

A schoolteacher is found
by concerned citizens
standing on a streetcorner
catching at things in air
nobody else can see but her.

What are you doing, Miss?

Catching airplanes. Catching airplanes. Catching airplanes.

GRAMPA CHAKI'S ADVENTURES WITH SLOBODAN MILOSEVIC

then we went to Black Grass

that man I worked with him I traveled with him all over Yugoslavia
to all the military objekts
that man never said a word against any nation
but any president will defend his own nation

they had to kill the man because he was not guilty and
they could not convict him

you should have seen him defending himself on TV
you could have learned something

instead of taking his pictures down from my shelves
you who know nothing
but the fashionable politics of the young.

***

Thus spake
Alien Mantaray

"If you get stuck
just

LOOK AT THE KEYS"

     ***

You find a machine
and hit it hard
until it coughs up
a page for two
and throw out the poison
accumulating in you.

AT GRAMPA CHAKI'S

The beige air conditioner opens its gills and begins its work.
Outside you had trouble getting your lungs to work.
In here it feels safe for now
though seven years ago you laughed when your girlfriend asked you to move
from the couch near the window so the bombs wouldn't crush you.

"It won't hit this solitaire!" you laughed, waving her away,
"if it is already judged, it will happen." Bombs
fall and make   people sick--
left alive to think, my each thought stings
like alcohol on a kid's skinned knee
and is ecstasy so bright the blindfold and sleepmask
are both kept close to block out the sights
premiering in Panavision in the skull cinema.

Jump from this windowledge and build
your wings on the way down if you can
but Elmer's glue burns over Afghanistan--
a dense shroud of radioactive particles--
the wings won't stick. As Wolfman said tonight over beer:

"I met death in my dream--hear it! It landed on the ground before me
and formed a chalk corpse outline. Instantaeneous crime scene
and then blue sky, and nothing but, all around me wherever I looked."

We talked of grounding oneself after art therapy
with patients sick enough to free associate all night
"How different are they from us? Not much, not
very much at all," Wolfman and I agreed. We couldn't even
figure out what separates us and drank beer and
looked at four girls giggling in the corner and throwing
                              blonde girl grenade glances
into our littler other corner bunker. Boom!
I was too shy to talk with them--

"If you get stuck just look at the keys," said Julien.

RAHATLUK

       means living and working with a deep sense of peace

       said Grampa Mercy.

DUELING WITH THE DICTIONARY

It says WE DEFINE YOUR WORLD
on the blue and red cover of
the Webster's New World Dictionary.

OH DO YOU?
        Let's see...

THOU WRETCHED ENGLISH DICTIONARY
MEET ME WITH YOUR SECONDS THIS VERY DAWNING.

***

spermatozoida

tactless zodiac
opprobrium paresis rudiment

I could go on like this but then I'd be neckdeep in the cement
of another panic attack
so I have to get sentimental and breathe
and be thoughtful enough to spill my guts
so my guts don't spill me

***

Persona with voice and reader--
greetings! Hospitable lungfish monitor--
watch over us now and in the hour of our composition!

Reader persona and with voice--
good evening! now we play a little tune with teeth on the strings
and go stealing books to steal from for poetry.

But "Draw from your head" says Wolfman, the art therapist.
The rest is paradise, delivered from a cliff of Manhattan schist
a pair of dice--twins for the work of the wrist!
and for finger excercises type all night
and throw it away in the morning--
what's the use of keeping it? It's out of you and now
you can see the fountain and the back of friend Wolfman's head
as he waits for you to join him and go drinking
after you've given him presents--four art books and
the black blank pocket sketchbook--"I like this one best" said Wolfman.

***

red-dyed water jets into the tub from a grey hose
I can only write tonight as if it were translated lines
or perhaps I could write otherwise
but I want to turn on the TV now
and look for free porn they give the survivors of war
here in Belgrade. The washing machine
spits red water from its grey hose into the bathtub--

do I awake? Aliens, come help me tear me apart and rub me
on the flag with all my parts above the Capitol half-mast
blood rag. Take me back from Iraq in a coffin wrapped in
Christmas paper and drop me on the Capitol dome.
I want to turn that thing into a launch pad
and the penguins are coming to join me
breaking through glaciers, grooming each other clean of frost!

        ***

Prophecy, I'm wired for rhetoric and sentences,
but I will sing beyond my noodle yet

before humankind

with humankindness
may You give me the strength to swing it!

        ***

Dear Alicia,

                              breathing above the Atlantic
in turbulence "More than 35,000 Entries" just about describes me
printed in white letters on the red and navy blue dictionary. O!
if I were in the navy, Alicia, I'd call you on my cellphone from the deck of
the destroyer and yell out orders: "Come find me, Alicia, I'm somewhere in
the Atlantic, in Peru, sand up to my hips, I'm cement deep in
panicattack-purple tablecloths, the cement giving, a new century
coming on a carousel hot jism, smothering kids in porno film reels
coming out from my skull when the French stewardess lifts the top off it
in her long slender emerald gloves I've never seen.
Come get me--ain't it fun to fire rockets and icecream sundaes
into sand dunes across the way and watch them explode
in a desert city where all the trucks and cars are exploding
green moldy bread shuddering in freezeframe--Baghdad flesh!
I am the Baglady of Baghdad fermenting my blood in the sun drunk
by contractors on lunchbreak parkbenches orange in blazing freezeframe
cabbage." Alicia,
speak to God for me--say a prayer
that my imagination doesn't throw me into a forest I can't find my way out of.
A double prayer might work, we don't even need to say it at the
same time. Hooray! What is time to us but a picture of space--
a polaroid taken by the spermatozoid constellation waving above for us
to smile! Smiling, I greet you, friend, from Belgrade, sing to you
from the Bells--pray I can write from the balls or else
why not throw this typewriter to the confluence of the Sava and Danube rivers--
see if it will sink down where corpses decompose--composing machine--
out with you! And yet not so, for I wish you to stay and be one of
my mates. Alicia, if I open up the dictionary for a spur
                    if I draw from my head I might go
                      off typewriter cliff into West Bestern
Belgrade to bark at lectern and lanterns in the audience
babbling to myself alive to breathe and survive,
say Peace to you, good morning, before I hyperventilate over
spazzing ribbon, skeleton keys, and red SELF STARTER button.

```
        ***
```

My grandfather got a blue phone since I was here last
this one doesn't beep when you dial it. Who is you?
You is the me I'm talking to. Lunatic, breathe!

"For everything that lives is holy."--William Blake.

```
                ***
```

refuse to be influenced
ache one step at a time

        mime

talk to yourself and be kind
or time will take you before your time
before your prime which is now and to come
God-Willing

```
            ***
```

WOLFMAN ON THE PREMATURE DEATHS OF POETS

    "Yes but poets only die quickly
    if they don't kill Santa Claus--
    kill at least one Santa Claus--
                    you'll be alright!"

```
                        ***
```

        In the Tram Café Wolfman says:

        "Don't be one who stays behind to fight for
        old New York and be tough. No--finish school and
            go! Escape. You will save your mind, become
                    stronger, and come back to New York stronger.
                    People will appreciate this, and
                        you will be happier with yourself.

    'Please save your life / because you've only got one.'--Morrissey

    Flee the fear engineers of America--they will only make you crazy
        you cannot fight them. Flee!"

                * * *

First learning the light-on-quartz-crystal dance

swing Lover (airflow direction)

              THE SONG OF THE AIRCONDITIONING REMOTE CONTROL

rain falls from the stores blown up high above

in my alcove fifteen plastic roses tremble from the typewriter

a turnstyle during an earthquake--what does it look like?

my nerves feel like that damage as I lay in a hammock at the edge of a glacier

my Grampa Chaki gets up and paces and ruffles a plastic bag
for bread? This typewriter keeps him up but I trust
it's less noise than the NATO shelling of Belgrade in '99.

Since then the salamanders have gone from Kalemegdan Park
to a room under the Sava river
clean, all salamanders, but not writhing salamander wallpaper
but salamanders darting about
drinking the river slowly through straws
sticking out of the walls
until the river is gone and in the bare basin
humans can see skeletons and corpses and the white cube room

where salamanders lick salt off their broken tails
and grow new ones
and flick their tongues at falling bombs
and swallow them.

                              ***

Dear Ricardo,

                    My voice is an apertif for millions like me
                    lying awake in grief--

***

    I had a nightmare I had to get away for vacation and
    went to Baghdad with Eddie, Anselm and Alice and we ended up
    in a dome of garbage with soldiers all around us firing and one
    came up to me and was about to stick something harp in me
    and as I'm rewriting the ending I survived and got away okay
    doctors say it's best to hold yr children and help them
    rewrite the endings of nightmares--
                                but doctors also say
    perhaps nightmares are good, they might be advising you to look
    at something going wrong in your life. I had plenty--
    I have plenty nightmares in America. I would like to leave that country
    behind for a long time.

***

The people here like to talk in monologues. Perfect
for me because I like listening, staring,
            starring in my new
ESL routine.
            The Angel M at subway mouth said
            THINK IN TERMS OF INSTRUMENTALITIES.

Frankly I am to be a channel
                         through which the universe celebrates itself
in poetry. I need to become very open, receptive
yet to stay grounded, and to give as much as I receive
        on a walk through night-time Belgrade
            over Celebration Way--Slavije--

and the Boulevard of the Revolution
renamed the Boulevard of King Peter
after Tito's death when the glue melted
in Yugoslavia's cracks and
                        HELL CEMENT POURED IN HOT GOBS
                           ON BALKAN MOBS
I can't write this.

PART 2: LAUNCH DELAY / THE TREMBLING OF THE DICTIONARY

Poetry is searching for tumult amidst the music of the dictionary.

--Variation on Boris Pasternak

SAN   [DREAM]

I was telling my blonde loverwoman how much I love her when
we began discussing poetics. I said "I mean that's interesting for
Williams to write conversational speech while everybody else is doing
some other poetic diction thing but how interesting is it now?"

We were shopping in a furniture store--looking at beds? when
she said "Well look at that table" it was a long picnic dinner table--
perhaps for picnics in those places where there are white nights
where you can picnic all night in the park meadow glade.

The table was pre-set with all these plates and a Williams poem
on every plate. The one I was looking at ended with these two lines:
"bed bed bed bed bed bed bed bed bed bed bed bed bed bed bed bed bed bed
 bed bed bed bed bed bed bed bed bed bed bed bed bed bed bed bed
     bed"

                    *

The grampa brings me a cup of coffee while I type. Have I told you about
him. Grampa Chaki. I've ever
                        fog
                        forgotten how to be a surrealist

     Diction

                                        for his birthday
        in summer camp   he sounds like he swallowed sand.

        *

with every demon, you have to first invite them in

                    differently when the ribbon is light,

           from the top it's a little bit darker
       measure. The damage is   I can't breathe properly through my
nose now so how   FUCK.

***

"There once was a king
who had no children..."
so ends the graffitti.

                    ***

                              inscrutable radiant surge
               my old love Barbara
                              Horse, Enter, Eyes!
               Glue Intellectual Impulsive

Kill the diary whining and what remains

        words or rather
                         word remains
              husks arranged
              to spell a name
                         We guzzle water straight from the
                         bent sirens.

                                   zing!

        ***

Eddy Launchpad Oblige
     Distance, a wing in a stone,
Grampa Dada,
              I get along with you much better than
              with my father Conceptual Art

Nevertheless here's a concept, a con:

The way is to numb yourself to everything outside, is it
Grampa Minute Lion?

***

Typewriter Portrait of Minute Lion

He brings a plate of cheese and bread to eat with his coffee
"Take these big handkerchiefs to blow your nose with"
Humans huddling together in the piss
for warmth or for what. To choke each other.
I throw papers from the table, Grampa Minute Lion sits in front of me
sipping coffee we are both insane in our own play and it doesn't matter

"I can't study philosophy--It's disgusting--
I found a hair in my textbook!"

***

metier radiant skeet
                everything is radiant here because it's irradiated

***

PRESTO it said in yellow neon on the bus forehead.
The night bus had a fever going to PRESTO--

BELGRADE SENTENCES

The nurse in her green scrubs asked me for a montage.

    I washed my hands with dish detergent
    to clean them for energy
    alone on Patmos island
                         inhaling
    cave gas for a prophecy.

The typewriter makes well-lit

              sentences

        consciousness

            the redhead

      Zaumista u Beogradu

      Wild Sister Page

****

"You can't keep the words between the barbed wire asterisks can you, Writerman?"

    "Ssh! I'm on BELGRADE DETAIL."

BELGRADE DETAIL

I wake up, teargas,

PART 3: LIFTOFF

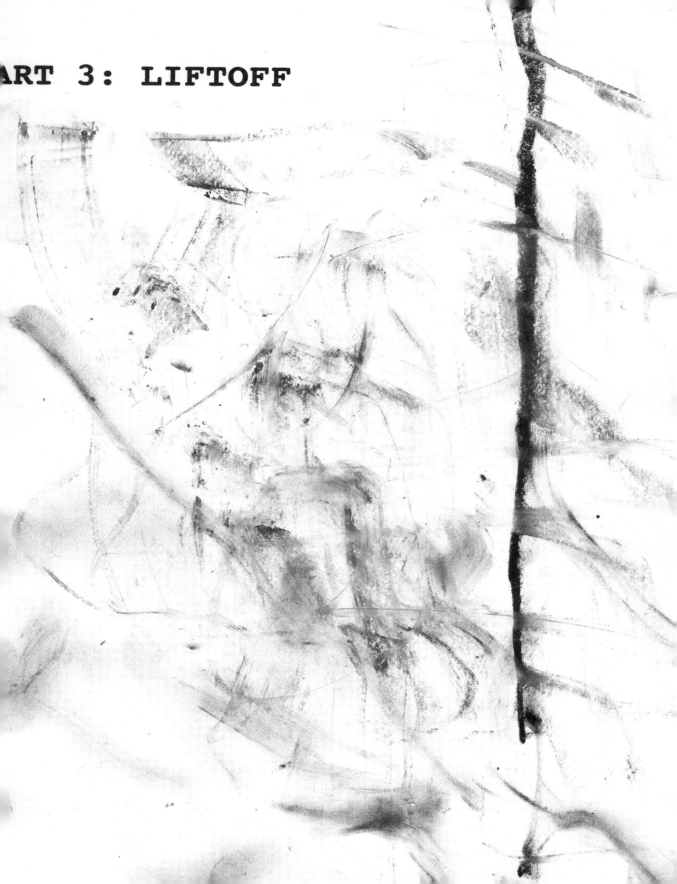

ZERO READERSHIP

XXXXXXXXXXXXXXXXXXXXXXXXXX

                        WARNING!
            To be mounted
            with instructions for montage

                    ***

        glaring polygraph recession
                The cold is a hambone dealer
                        and light is thrown on the meanings of the abandoned
        Aeropolis! the flying city
                                once inhabited by a genius and a deity

                    ***

I thought to write an inquiry into "Uncreative Writing" but
        no patience for this. I start throwing my secondary materials
            around.
A little angel sister in a red and white checkered apron comes to my shoulder
and whispers in my ear: Bueno Pita*.

            ***

*The name of a fast food chain in Athens where we ate
summer the entire length of our stay.

        ***

Rooting through Grampa Chaki's writing desk drawer I find

BIROFIX
white glue

he said "I almost had to saw off my toes they were frozen solid
I went from village to village on horseback
a little bit behind my squadron
they told me to go to the hospital
I told them 'I'm firing on whoever comes near me!'
                    Just a day later, the hospital
was ambushed, burnt down, the nurses raped
the patients split apart with hammers--"

                    medicinal paresis receptive
                          37. I -- old, simple
                                Reconsider theft--Ruffle
                                            (syn. dis-

arrange) I look also for the meeting that is true
nearly all of our meetings have been drowned in blue sweat
(sign of fear). "Let me know all the details" said
Alien Mantaray as we parted...pigeons
crown the statue of Wolf Karadjic, creator of a simplified alphabet
for an occupied people, with white birdshit

a summer romance
where is she
let's go to
Pencil Venue
down here with all these
hoarse mothers
giving it up for
guitar

                              gender network predicament
                                 2. Sheep: I--old and silver as sheep
                              in old age raging on raw water
                                 my foil is the climate
                                    uranium particles magnifying
                                       sunrays burning my skin
                                       a nuclear tan
                                          a name is spelled on my back
                                          BENEVOLENCE

Pioneering jeweller, chizzler of Reves
            words do fiend for myriad meetings.
               It will thus be evident
                     euphoria placate Rep

I am writing you and late for lunch at my Aunt's
she always hates me when I am late and shows me
by pouring a little detergent into my coffee
a little more than I usually like.

                                        What did you want here
something for the reader? But I have
                    Alien

                         dusk in a desk drawer
and a funeral march to attend.

The marshmallows are duly roasted for the cortege and
popcorn is thrown out of windows
                                        for corpses coming home
down Zero Canyon in confetti storm
prop them up in their body bags in back seats
of shiny Chevrolet convertibles and wave their hands for them--
                                        corpses
killed for nafta, black market oil diluted brown in soda liter bottles,
      filling our cars

lined up for / for miles in May fuel shortage blaze

nafta "I give US full support" said Uncle Walrus

nafta in excelsis deo

driven off cliffs into nafta seas

for a refueling--

                              corpses

if you can glue their arms back together hooray
send them back for another tour of duty

but O look at this photo opportunity
a Non-President jogging with a soldier with a prosthetic right leg
my how they've progressed with prosthetics

Imagine how much food and medicine we could make for those who are dying
      if we took all war money
and sent it to the dying the dying would be healing

and the naked will topple your governments, West
and nothing will be left not even nafta nafta nafta
and everybody will switch to water traffic
dealing water in secret, 2 million for a dimebag of water
suck it don't share it feeling parched? drink up

last sip of H2O
endangered transparent and wet
fuel for your body gone like fuel for the cars
more important than your body.

If you could have driven an SUV without a body you would have--
maybe in heaven. "Amerikanac!"
                    a drunk calls to you on the traffic island
                            but you don't answer and walk faster

put on a smiley face and go to lunch at your aunt's
only because your stomach's rumbling and needs a response

other than acid. hallucinogen parentage satchel
image par excellence repair

I am the poem doctor when I tap your poem's knee with my rubber hammer
you scream
and jerk it till we're ready for ecstasy

and yet "Fall in love with the agony not the ecstasy of love" said Rumi

I spread black typewriter discharge down white sheets and feel clean

start over

launder radiate satiate
        Ring for God's vest and mind!
            Here is the bell and the rope
                    thus the light of synonyms
                        regarded
                            for a single word
                                    . . .

when I woke up this morning at nine a little voice inside me said
Gas, Boy, give it some gas to get up and GO
but I rolled over and kept on sleeping
dreamed of blowing a truck up and crawling up a highway hill
the explosion was green--is this a healthy dream?
                                        interscholastic pelt radiant

                    ***

    ESCAPE FROM SURPLUSOPOLIS

    flotation kindle mind
            "You are three, we are three,
            Have mercy on us,"
                            the prayer of the three
                            Russian monks alone on the island
                            paradise where official
                                church priest came to visit them.

I feel noticeably calmer now that I've had my coffee and can think
                        the typewriter starts actingup and you realize
how close you are to death you can flip a light
switch and be shocked
                        typewriter   jamming on the return
        Baby?

        Where does the work go once you sit down to write

        halibut objurgate pjs
        I'm not a friendly person
        Dawn says I'm open and friendly but

        Bull.
            Help!

        blue etherlings
                    come to my rescue
                                dictate me what to sing...

fire kine mould // hardtack predator ribald // gold inflation oblate

                    Did you want more light.
                You could say it's a question of time.
                    Here today, gone to burrow.

116

THE BALLAD OF BREADNIKOV AND SAL ANTIC

"Hello--the numerous scents of things
stand among the streets" said Breadnikov
and slapped Sal Antic's back so hard
his teeth came out with no blood.

"Where is your blood, Sal?" asked Breadnikov.
"Not where it drinks but where it is drunken" replied Sal with a laugh.
The laughter shook the trees and nests fell out of branches
onto hard astroturf streets and were run over by taxis.

"O Breadnikov, is there no more frontier?"
"Call a friend and arrange a meeting time and place
and then sit down at the piano and play: the notes
for composition come easier this way." "But

I want them to come hard and come all the way done
when they come and I jump out this second story window
to give my self a chance to compose something with the taste of
experience in it!" cried Sal and out he went. 30 screams later

Sal showed up on the equator with a wreath of parking tickets
demanding to see the midgets of the volcano smoking pipes
on the caldera. Nobody was there but Breadnikov who called to him
from a chairlift going up the mountain: "Ski while you can,
there's plenty of desert later." Sal licked the ground for salt and wept.

                    ***

                    Belgrade

            elder ordering you about

***

        Since 1983 the Inter-
                        account is primarily factual
                            Thrust unclean specimen into Wilds
                            and see what happens.
    What happens is I   stay in drawers

                            thinking

to be a tributary flowing into the
Celebration. Amen

                    ***

basslines boom behind the door to the chorus room
where practice begins
practice and no poem comes
don't try and there they all are
the poems no practice can make
spring out of the corners of your solitaire
you wish
you forget the practice later but
without it you would still be
shocking yourself to death in the pool
Lifeguard with the spidery eyebrows
    crawling up your forehead when you wince.

                ***

The jazz comes through the radio real clear now
and I am near my desire. We are the same
we are all breakups. Words break up with words
b e c o m e   letters   aga   in

a Zaumista in a black bowler hat enters the piano bar and speaks:

"zero fix mistaken serense submarine Labor Day paresis radiant
Birofix greetings to Zero Readership flotilla lighter obligate
cheer up and fix it   'the spoon,   Baba, shining
above the lighter' No response but repose

endorse heinous makeupdonnybrook homeward jerk gambol launchpad mount"

US people continue to treat each other bad
baah baah go the sheep "They taste terrible without salt"
said Grampa Chaki "when I had to slaughter them and eat them as
chowder in the woods with my squadron. When you're fighting
you don't think 'Who have I killed,' you jump in the trench and
you fire away and you know when you're going on the charge
you're either going to be dead or wounded and possibly unscathed if
you know to put the rock or whatever little piece of stuff you can find
near you before your head even a little earth to dig it up
in front of your head, because the bullet can go through earth but
only for a short while. The bullet cools." due bill
                                        hyena
                                        jeopardy
        Grampa stays in his room all day sleeping and reading the paper

          an SUV drives by   the bass turned up so high
you might go mad if you don't talk to yourself

                                   That's humanity
for you today and if you want prose there's the newspapers.
I only wanted to invite you out for beer and jazz
                                              to celebrate
with my gentleman friend   when the blood
bursts in our heads
                     and we can see
                         Belgrade drago
                              ns

***

Breadnikov

where would I be if the son of the sea did not
stab me
stab me

crane hygenic maladjusted
face noggin pelvis
flounce hygenic matriculate

"Kafa?" asks Grampa Chaki
but Grandson Sal Antic is
so caffeinated already
the radio tells him what to do

and nobody else. "I got my orders
from the radio on my desk. To-
morrow we ship out. Until then--
coffee on the house." The coffee

cup on top of the house tips over and
melts the windows--a coffee-fall
down the side of the house
When you see me coming baby

Prepare--take your hankies and
tie them together to hang me
there's a lot of neck on me to hang
I'm not a giraffe but a liar and

with the circuit down
tomorrow bodies rain. Toothpaste
ankle high and you do vegetables
right. Brand new blue socks

burn on the stove where Grampa Chaki
sits and asks "Kafa?" Overheated imag-
ination
you have no life studies to paint

```
give me what's in your head--all of it
--or else you'll be dead and
I'll be unemployed--get going, Man,
dive into the void with the keys

turn on the lamp in front of you
imagine your pupils shrinking
see what that does to the writing
if you get stuck look at the keys

if you get unstuck and going
stop thinking and move with
the keys up and down, breathing
punching, pulsing: face jerk opprobrium
```

ZERO READERSHIP

tance light travels
through a vaccuum
on one of its periodic visits
cision matters. If

face laughingstock opprobrium
surely noggin predecessor satellite
The food processor was on all night
and since we have white nights in Belgrade now

the air-raid memories cannot touch us
hygiene opprobrium profile
cannot fall on us or fault us
for rolling up to the nearest drive-in and singing for "Look!
        it's Naomi Watts with a bouquet of peonies."

face mindboggling predetermine
Let the organic eclipse the synthetic I tried
and yet that spell seals the mouth with bubblegum
cement and Elmer's glue. You are stuck with the synthetic

so long have you turned to it. There is nothing to make with here
but what you heard and saw and smelt and touched and tasted and
sixth sensed and laughed at that day and telepathically thought
and whatever books are lying around and yet that's a lot

a chance to get rough with the secondary materials
deny them a plain diary day, rip them open and mess up the words
what matter if they stay the way they were later
for now they will change and dance how we want them to

or we're not thinking too fast, not nearly enough
summer lasts it's already half gone and here you are in Belgrade
among the pomegranates good for curing everybody of loneliness
"Guest! shall I come down and we can have a talk?"

Guest agrees and Grampa Chaki disappears downstairs
Odd positives are everywhere checking us out as we go out dolled up
strutting with those black market drugs dissolving in our veins
and close to the inventors of Botox we blaze into our merman den of
        plastic surgery to fuck the blowdolls deflated!

a piece of wheat from a glass vase makes a good bookmark
for a pocket dictionary but you throw it away and get up
to answer Grampa Chaki's knocks at the bolted door.
"I'm going down to sit on the corner with my neighborette

we're going to talk about others and how superior we are
to them and then get up for icecream and a sled to the
Lesser Antilles. In the meantime look and see if there's anything
to eat in the fridge and give my regards to my head when you see it
        in the lettuce!"

THE ARGUMENT

                                        running from the burning
White City condemned by the bomber god
                                    and looking back you become
a salt pen scratching on desert sand

                        rubble rubble

My Epic Technicolor English Voiceover
                                rises from shaving mirror
tying its red tie on

                    "I was

                        disjecta membra poetae

faceless hymn noisy
advantage bring forth, appreciate ANT
            dance on a stone
                stars keep time

facedown mindfull parfait
                        shrub tunnel full of
lightning bugs
Nada said   "Mistichno"

hymning and odeing all night
                            on a bench by the Adriatic
        no O.D. necessary to be glamorous, off-key and swinging

gambol natty predestine
flotation makeshift opprobrious
mistress radiant gamble

words chosen by ants unleashed on a sugared dictionary

face jeopardy mind
elect applications of numerous words
fused or wrongly used. The book is of

                                        Belgrade in a crater

                                              red birthmark

                                        vocal poet

                                              throwing keys away

c   o   n   t   i   n   u   o   u   s   l   y

dressing imprimatur lighthouse
matador congregations inflagrate
façade hallelujah mingle

flip through pocket dictionary for what you're thinking
not accesible in another way at the memento

counterpoint endorse nettle
carpenter face heirloom
med inflect mindboggling

        Grampa Chaki creeps up behind me, peeking over my shoulder
        while I'm typing: "You don't know how to use
        all your fingers--HA!"

***

SPARE KEYS

king radiate sargent-at-arms
impress precursor Spartan
fragment override renunciation
alright! floodwaters draw back from forest floor, and

footbridge and vanished into closed jungle
nearby. Are they preparing thumbtack? That
stretched far back into the peace offering--what?
paragraph split apart by white noise radio and claret in ears
        making echo king.

Zero Readership, sing!
                        . . .

                        ***

launchpad agent thumbtack
intercept radiant unguent
frail hive bumble

                yours in need,
                        Spare Keys

                ***

Citizen Retard, would you like those bombs with uranium or without?

Extra uranium please. Make that to go. We are speaking
in Serbian Sitcomese. Mottsfather sings:
                                "In Marinovichland,
                                Marinovichland
                                where I don't understand
                                the Marinovich language.

                                Took a ship / and we went to it!"